Hezbollah

Author: Rice, Earle.

Lexile Value: 1250L

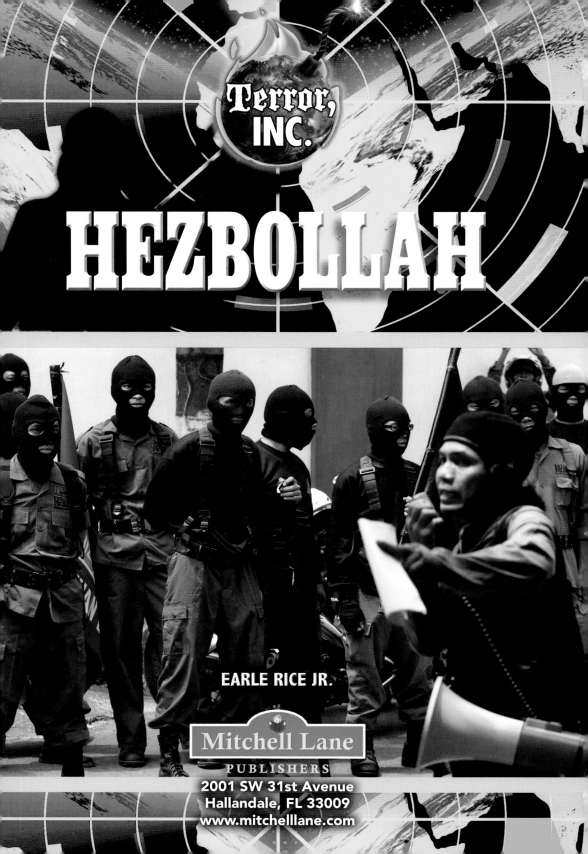

Terror, INC.

HEZBOLLAH

EARLE RICE JR.

Mitchell Lane
PUBLISHERS
2001 SW 31st Avenue
Hallandale, FL 33009
www.mitchelllane.com

Printing   1   2   3   4   5   6   7   8

Al-Qaeda
Boko Haram
Hamas

Hezbollah
Islamic State
Muslim Brotherhood

ABOUT THE COVER: Black-masked, uniformed members of the Organization of Islamic Jihad gather for a demonstration in Surakarta, in central Java, Indonesia, in April 2014.

ABOUT THE AUTHOR: Earle Rice Jr. is a former senior design engineer and technical writer in the aerospace, electronic-defense, and nuclear industries. He has devoted full time to his writing since 1993, specializing in military and counterinsurgency subjects. Earle is the author of more than 80 published books. He is listed in *Who's Who in America* and is a member of the Society of Children's Book Writers and Illustrators, the League of World War I Aviation Historians, the Air Force Association, and the Disabled American Veterans.

Library of Congress Cataloging-in-Publication Data
Names: Rice, Earle, author.
Title: Hezbollah / by Earle Rice Jr.
Description: Hallandale, FL : Mitchell Lane Publishers, [2018] | Series: Terror INC |
   Includes bibliographical references and index.
Identifiers: LCCN 2017009124 | ISBN 9781680200539 (library bound)
Subjects: LCSH: Hizballah (Lebanon)—Juvenile literature.
Classification: LCC JQ1828.A98 R54 2018 | DDC 324.25692/082—dc23
LC record available at https://lccn.loc.gov/2017009124

eBook ISBN: 978-1-68020-054-6

Contents

Words in **bold** throughout can be found in the Glossary.

Foreword

Terror has plagued the world since men in caves flailed away at each other with sticks and stones. As the world emerged from **primeval** times and entered the ancient age, humans clashed on a larger, more advanced scale called warfare. Slings, arrows, and spears wrought havoc in the Golden Age of Greece and stained the glory that was Rome. Ethnic and religious strife followed close behind. In medieval times, crusading Christians and faith-based Muslims carved a bloody path across the Middle East with sword, lance, and scimitar in the causes of God and Allah. Americans engaged in "total war" for the first time during the Civil War, a war pitting brother against brother and fathers against sons at a cost of 750,000 lives. The 20th century introduced global wars that claimed the lives of tens of millions of combatants and civilians.

Today, international terrorism has become a form of warfare. The U.S. Department of Defense defines terrorism as "the unlawful use of—or threatened use of—force or violence against individuals or property to **coerce** or intimidate governments or societies, often to achieve political, religious, or **ideological** objectives." In many parts of the world, terror is a way of life. Militant Muslim extremists seek to rid Muslim countries of what they view as the **profane** influence of the West and replace their governments with fundamentalist regimes based on their interpretation of the religion of **Islam**.

The American way of life changed forever when 19 Islamist terrorists flew fuel-laden aircraft—flying bombs—into the World Trade Center in New York City and the Pentagon in Washington,

Lebanese women and children celebrate Israel's release of five Lebanese prisoners and the bodies of 199 fighters in the southern suburbs of Beirut in July 2008. An exchange agreement between Lebanon and Israel returned the bodies of Ehud Goldwasser and Eldad Regev, two soldiers who had been captured two years earlier. Notable among the returned Lebanese prisoners was Samir Kantar, who had been held for nearly 30 years in an Israeli jail. He had been serving three life sentences for a 1979 triple murder.

DC, on September 11, 2001. Today, radical Islamist groups continue to be America's main threat of terrorism.

It should be noted that only a small minority of Muslims believe in terror as a strategy. A recent Gallup poll indicated that just seven percent of the world's 1.6 billion Muslims support extremist views of terrorism. The purpose of this book is to alert and enlighten the reader about that seven percent, while affirming the essential righteousness of the other 93 percent of Islam's followers. Peace be upon the gentle of mind, spirit, and deed.

The earth shook and a billowing black cloud climbed high above the headquarters and barracks of a unit of U.S. Marines following a truck-bomb explosion that killed 241 men in Beirut, Lebanon, on October 23, 1983.

CHAPTER 1
Cast in Fire

Beirut, Lebanon. Sunday, October 23, 1983. Marines of the First Battalion, Eighth Marines—Battalion Landing Team (BLT) 1/8—were quartered at the Beirut International Airport in an abandoned four-story building. They formed a part of the 24th Marine Amphibious Unit (MAU). The building also served as Marine headquarters. Earlier, it had housed the Lebanese Aviation Administration Bureau, the Palestine Liberation Organization (PLO), Syrians, and Israelis. The Israelis had used the building as a field hospital during their invasion that June. Strategically positioned, it stood between Israeli units to the south and east of the airport and Muslim neighborhoods to the north.

At 0500, Lance Corporal Eddie DiFranco was standing watch at Post Number 6 in the parking lot in front of BLT headquarters. He watched curiously as a yellow stake-bed Mercedes-Benz truck—similar to vehicles that carried water—drove into the parking area, circled the lot, and left. An hour or so later, Lance Corporal John Berthiame at Post Number 5 observed a white Mercedes sedan on the nearby airport highway, moving slowly past the headquarters building. "[T]he guy driving," he recalled later, "reached out . . . and took two pictures of the building, and I thought that was kind of strange."[1]

At about 0620, a yellow truck—almost certainly the same one DiFranco had seen earlier—drove into the parking lot. It was packed with the military explosive PETN—equal to more than six tons of TNT. (PETN, or pentaerythritol tetranitrate, is a highly explosive organic compound in the nitroglycerin family.) In a burst of speed, it crashed through a five-foot-high wire barrier,

careened through an open gate, smacked down the Sergeant of the Guard's sandbagged booth at the building's entrance, hurtled into the lobby, and detonated in a flash of light and a thunderous roar.

The force of the blast lifted the entire structure, blew out the concrete pillars on the ground floor, and collapsed the upper 50 feet of the building into a pile of rubble about 20 feet high. Scores of dead and wounded Marines lay sandwiched between the crumpled floors and ceilings. Examiners at the scene described the blast as perhaps the largest manmade, non-nuclear explosion in history.

The blast claimed the lives of 241 American servicemen: 220 Marines, 18 sailors, and three soldiers. Another 128 Americans suffered wounds. It marked the deadliest single-day death toll for the U.S. Marine Corps since the first day of fighting on Iwo Jima in World War II.

At virtually the same time, a similar explosion toppled the nine-story Drakkar building about four miles away. It was home to the French First Parachute Chasseur Battalion. The blast killed 58 paratroopers and wounded 15 more. The casualty count represented France's worst military loss since the fighting ended in Algeria in 1962.

Both the Marines and the French paratroopers constituted elements of the Multinational Force (MNF). The MNF was an international peacekeeping force at the height of the Lebanese Civil War. It also included units from the United Kingdom and Italy. The bombings eventually led to the withdrawal of the MNF.

Though shocked by the Beirut bombings, few Americans grasped the significance of the twin blasts. A deadly new form of terror—on a scale never seen before—emerged from the dust and rubble of the MNF installations. Speaking later at a memorial service, Marine commandant General James Amos said, "The world we live in and what we knew of the future security environ-

British soldiers lend a hand evacuating victims from the bombed-out wreckage of the Marine headquarters building in Beirut. Almost 25 years later, Hezbollah announced that Imad Mughniyeh, the suspected mastermind of the attack, had been killed. Mughniyeh was accused of many other attacks that killed hundreds of Americans and Israelis.

ment was forever changed. It was a new way to attack the West. It was a cowardly attack on freedom."[2]

Evidence soon surfaced linking the bombings to a newly formed terrorist group known as Hezbollah (pronounced hehz-buh-LAH, Arabic for "Party of Allah" or "Party of God"). The group took its name from a passage in the Quran, the holy book

of the religion of Islam, describing who will triumph over infidels (non-believers): "Allah has inscribed the Faith on their very hearts and strengthened them with a spirit of His own. He will admit them to gardens watered by running streams, where they shall dwell forever. Allah is well pleased with them and they with Him. They are confederates of Allah: and Allah's confederates shall surely triumph."[3]

Hezbollah, a **Shia** organization, was further known to be created, supported, financed, and directed by the Shia regime of Iran. Colonel Timothy Geraghty, the commanding officer of the targeted Marine BLT in Beirut, later wrote:

> Unknown to us at the time, the National Security Agency had made a diplomatic communications intercept on 26 September . . . in which the Iranian Intelligence Service provided explicit instructions to the Iranian ambassador in Damascus (a known terrorist) to attack the Marines at Beirut International Airport. The suicide attackers struck us 28 days later, with word of the intercept stuck in the intelligence pipeline until [three] days after the attack.[4]

Hezbollah had emerged from a loose coalition of radical Shia groups during the Israeli incursion into southern Lebanon in 1982. Most of those groups were breakaways from the more moderate Amal movement. They consisted mainly of a Shia underclass hoping to assert economic and political power for the first time. Inspired by the Iranian Revolution three years earlier, Hezbollah arose out of Iran's efforts to assemble the militant Shia groups in Lebanon under one umbrella. It also owed its origins to Israel's attempt to break up the Palestine Liberation Organization (PLO) by its incursion into Lebanon.

Former Israeli prime minister Ehud Barak noted many years later, "When we entered Lebanon . . . there was no Hezbollah. We

A group of 1,284 Hezbollah members raise their arms in a salute to their leader Sheikh Hassan Nasrallah and vow to continue fighting at a Martyr's Day observance in Beirut, Lebanon, on November 11, 2001. The United States condemned the group, listing it as a terrorist organization and requesting a freeze on its assets. But the Lebanese government disagreed. It instead recognized Hezbollah as a legitimate resistance group and denied the U.S. request.

were accepted with perfumed rice and flowers by the Shia in the south. It was our presence there that created Hezbollah."[5]

Hezbollah was cast in fire. It led the armed resistance against the Israeli invasion and occupation of a large part of southern Lebanon throughout the 1980s and 1990s. It is widely credited with forcing Israel's eventual withdrawal in May 2000.

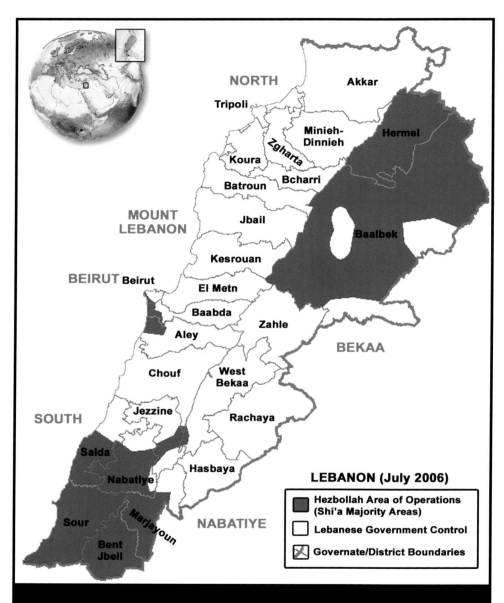

NORTH
Akkar
Tripoli
Minieh-
Dinnieh
Hermel
Zgharta
Koura
Bcharri
Batroun
MOUNT
LEBANON
Jbail
Baalbek
Kesrouan
BEIRUT Beirut
El Metn
Baabda
Aley
Zahle
BEKAA
Chouf
West
Bekaa
SOUTH
Jezzine
Rachaya
Saida
Hasbaya
Nabatiye
LEBANON (July 2006)
Marjayoun
NABATIYE
Sour
Bent
Jbeil

Hezbollah Area of Operations
(Shi'a Majority Areas)

Lebanese Government Control

Governate/District Boundaries

Much of the western world knows Hezbollah as a terrorist organization, but the group also holds seats in the government of Lebanon. In addition to its militant operations, it furthers its influence by operating hospitals, clinics, schools, and other social activities.

Amal Movement

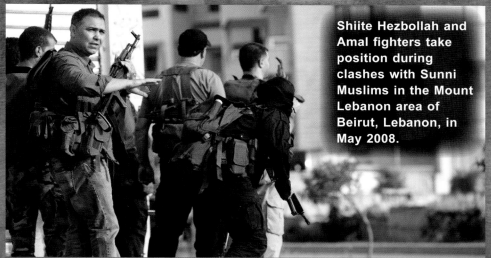

Shiite Hezbollah and Amal fighters take position during clashes with Sunni Muslims in the Mount Lebanon area of Beirut, Lebanon, in May 2008.

The Amal Movement is a Shia-associated political party and **militia** in Lebanon. In 1974, Imam Musa al-Sadr, an Iranian-born Shia cleric of Lebanese descent, founded the Movement of the Dispossessed. It was an organization dedicated to the **emancipation** of the Shia population. When civil war erupted in 1975, Sadr launched a military wing of the group and called it Amal, which means "hope" in Arabic. Amal is also an acronym for *Afwaj al-Muqawamah al-Lubnaniyah*, which translates to "Lebanese Resistance Brigades."

Amal's primary aim was to seek justice for all deprived Lebanese, particularly members of the Shia community. Though influenced by Islamic teachings, it operated as a **secular** movement. It tried to bring people together along communal rather than religious or ideological lines. But Sadr—who disappeared mysteriously while visiting Libya in 1978—also intended Amal to fight against Israel as part of the Lebanese army.

After Sadr's presumed death, other Lebanese armed factions became disenchanted with what they viewed as Amal's moderate policies. "As a result," notes Middle Eastern expert Matthew Levitt, "disaffected Amal members joined with other Shia militant groups—including the Muslim Students Union, the Dawa Party of Lebanon, and others—and established their own umbrella group, Hezbollah."[6]

Lebanese militiamen of Socialist leader Kamal Jumblatt wave their flag and brandish AK-47 semiautomatic rifles atop a captured army armored personnel carrier on the Beirut-Damour highway in January 1976. It was a time of continuing heavy clashes.

CHAPTER 2
Raison D'être

Hezbollah was founded in 1982, but its *raison d'être* (RAY-zohn DET-ruh)—French for "reason for being"—reaches much farther back into Lebanon's turbulent history.

Lebanon's population comprises 60 percent Muslims and 40 percent Christians. Christianity came to Lebanon about 325 CE (Common Era). Muslims from the Arabian Peninsula occupied Lebanon in 638. In time, Islam gradually replaced Christianity along Lebanon's coastal area, while Christians continued to thrive in the mountainous regions.

In 1095, Christians and Muslims took up sword and scimitar and fought each other for control of the Holy Land, which included Lebanon. Egyptian Mamluks finally drove out the last of the Christian crusaders in 1291. Slightly more than two centuries later, the Ottoman Empire—centered in what is today's Turkey—conquered Lebanon. Christians and Muslims lived together in relative peace during 500 years of Ottoman rule.

During World War I, the Ottoman Empire sided with Germany. When the conflict ended, the victorious French and British carved up much of the Ottoman territory. France took over Lebanon and Syria. In 1923, the **League of Nations** formally awarded the **mandate** for Syria and Lebanon to France. The French united the Christians and Muslims under one government and helped write Lebanon's constitution. Lebanon officially gained independence from France in 1943. Christians and Muslims agreed to share power in the government. Lebanon maintained ties with the West and prospered as a center of trade and finance.

But in 1958, political and religious differences in the country and Arab unrest in the region led to a largely Muslim rebellion against the government. President Camille Chamoun, fearing an overthrow of his Western-aligned government, called on the United States for help. The United States sent a contingent of Marines to Lebanon in July, 1958. Peace was restored and the Marines left in October. Their brief presence was a **precursor** of future U.S. involvement.

After Israel defeated the Arab armies of Syria, Jordan, and Egypt in the Six-Day War of 1967, thousands of Palestinian refugees flooded into Lebanon. In November, 1969, the Lebanese state and the PLO signed an understanding known as the Cairo Agreement. It granted the PLO the right to take part in the Arab struggle against Israel "in accordance with the principles of the sovereignty and security of Lebanon."[1]

The PLO is a political organization that represents the Palestinian people. It was founded in Jerusalem in 1964. Its aim is to establish an independent state for Palestinians. Elements of the PLO started to raid targets in Israel from bases in Lebanon. Israel responded to the PLO attacks with strikes against their forces in Lebanon. Muslims in Lebanon favored the PLO presence; Christians did not.

By 1974, Israeli incursions into Lebanon began occurring on an almost daily basis. Lebanese political leader Imam Musa al-Sadr started recruiting Shia volunteers for militia training in newly formed Amal camps. The training was conducted by Fatah, the armed military wing of the PLO. Meanwhile, Lebanon's growing Muslim population began to demand increased power in the government. Christians opposed their demands and resented the Muslim alliance with the PLO. On Sunday, April 13, 1975, PLO gunmen attempted to assassinate Maronite Christian Phalangist leader Pierre Gemayel as he was leaving church. (Maronites are the dominant Christian group in Lebanon; Phalangists are a

Christian political party and militia supported mainly by the Maronites.) In retaliation, Phalangist gunmen ambushed a bus in Beirut, killing 27 Palestinian refugees. Clashes between PLO/Muslim forces and Phalangists soon blossomed into a full-scale civil war.

On December 6, a day later remembered as "Black Saturday," four Christians were found dead in Beirut. Phalangists quickly sought reprisals. They set up roadblocks, stopped Muslim men, and murdered them on the spot. Muslim militias reciprocated. By day's end, some 300 Muslims and 300 Christians lay dead in the first major massacre of the war. From then on, both factions routinely killed civilians. This first phase of the Lebanese Civil War claimed many lives and caused widespread property damage.

Over the course of the drawn-out war, various factions of diverse interests would clash with one another. Opposing forces included Christians against the PLO and leftists, Christians vs. Syrians, Israelis vs. the PLO, Christians vs. Druze (Muslims) and Shia, Shia vs. Palestinians, even Christians vs. Christians.

The following June, Lebanon's President Suleiman Frangieh invited Syrian President Hafiz al-Assad to send troops into Lebanon. Syrian troops known as the Arab Deterrent Force (ADF) entered Lebanon. They came supposedly as peacekeepers, but also to aid Maronite Christians in their growing fight against leftist Muslim and Palestinian forces.

Some factions resented Syrian intervention and aligned themselves with Israel. Maronite priest Mansour Hokayem explained the situation in southern Lebanon: "We had a thousand shells raining on us. We had many casualties and they had to go to Israel. There was no escape for us. . . . We were pushed into Israel's arms."[2]

Israel served notice of things to come in March, 1978. In response to a Fatah commando operation that killed dozens of Israelis, the Israel Defense Forces (IDF) launched a brief incur-

Soviet-built tanks of the peacekeeping Syrian Army roll through the streets of Beirut in November, 1976. Lebanese teenagers exchange waves with peacekeeping soldiers on a mission to stop Lebanon's 19-month-long civil war.

sion into Lebanon. Before withdrawing six days later, the IDF spread destruction far and wide.

Three months later, Phalangists killed Frangieh's son Tony, along with his wife and daughter. Their murders ruled out any quick end to the civil war.

That August, the shadowy disappearance of Imam Musa al-Sadr left Shias ready for a new leader. Coincidentally, events were taking shape in Iran that would soon rock the entire Islamic world. In the eyes of various disparate Islamic radical groups, the yet-unborn Hezbollah was close to finding its raison d'être.

Terrorism

Viewpoints

On March 11, 1978, a Fatah raiding party in rubber dinghies landed on a beach in northern Israel. Led by 19-year-old female Dalal Mughrabi, the raiders killed an American photojournalist and a taxi driver, hijacked a bus, and commandeered another. Driving down the coastal highway, they set out on a bloody shooting rampage. Their melee left 38 Israelis dead, including 13 children. Mughrabi and eight other terrorists also died. The event became known as the Coastal Road Massacre.

Three days later, the Israel Defense Forces launched a seven-day offensive into Lebanon called Operation Litani. The Israelis occupied the area south of the Litani River with 25,000 troops. Their mission was to push Palestinian militant groups away from the border. It was also to bolster the South Lebanese Army (SLA), Israel's ally at the time.

Israeli Defense Minister Ezer Weizman said the invasion was intended to "clean up once and for all terrorist 'concentrations' in southern Lebanon."[3] But the terrorists retreated to the north, and the IDF found no such concentrations. The operation claimed the lives of about 1,100 Palestinians and Lebanese—about half of whom were Palestinian terrorists—and 23 Israeli soldiers. It also forced a mass exodus of many people living in the area.

Palestinians still laud Dalal Mughrabi as a valiant freedom fighter. Israelis remember her as a bloody terrorist. It's all in the point of view.

On March 11, 2010, Palestinians hold a banner with a picture of Palestinian militant Dalal Mughrabi as they protest in the West Bank city of Ramallah. The banner reads in Arabic: "Circle of marchers of Dalal Mughrabi. A promise is a promise, and an oath is an oath. The Palestine Liberation Movement."

UNIFIL troops scan the adjacent region from the roof of the Al Yatun Dutchblatt Position 7-16 in Lebanon in 1981. A U.S.-built Jeep and station wagon belonging to the HOPS 44 Armored Infantry of the Royal Netherlands Army are parked outside the station.

CHAPTER 3
In God's Name

The world was quick to condemn Israel's Operation Litani incursion into Lebanon. Three days after it began, the United Nations adopted Resolutions 425 and 426. Resolution 425 called for the immediate withdrawal of Israeli forces from Lebanon. Resolution 426 established the UN Interim Force in Lebanon (UNIFIL) to oversee the Israeli withdrawal. UNIFIL was originally deployed for six months, with an option to extend its stay if needed. It remains in Lebanon today.

Israel withdrew its forces, relying on the small Army of Free Lebanon led by Major Saad Haddad to secure a buffer zone between Israel and PLO operatives. Haddad's command consisted of a few hundred Maronites, Shia, Druze, and Phalangists. They formed the base of the future South Lebanese Army (SLA). Palestinian cross-border attacks followed by Israeli retaliation continued sporadically.

On January 16, 1979, Iranian ruler Mohammad Reza Shah Pahlavi fled his throne amid the chaos of the Iranian Revolution. Iranian cleric and revolutionary Ayatollah Ruhollah Khomeini returned from exile near Paris and set up a fundamentalist Islamic Shia **theocracy**. Iran immediately began exporting its revolution.

Two years later, Khomeini said that Iran needed to work harder to improve its world image in order to continue exporting its revolution. "We have been near zero in our propaganda abroad," he said. "If we want to export this revolution, we must do something so that the people themselves take government into their own hands."[1] He spoke in a Tehran radio broadcast that reported the execution of 20 **dissidents**.

Following the 1978 Israel invasion of Lebanon known as Operation Litani, the United Nations established a demarcation line between Lebanon and Israel called the Blue Line (shown in dark blue) after the Israeli withdrawal. It traced an earlier 1949 cease-fire line known as the Green Line, and followed the somewhat contested Lebanese-Syrian border toward the Israeli-occupied Golan Heights.

In July 1981, PLO militants launched another round of **Katyusha** rockets into northern Israel. The Israel Air Force (IAF) struck back by bombing PLO centers in the densely populated Fakhani district in Beirut. Scores of civilians died in the attacks. Undeterred, the PLO continued their rocket barrages. After two weeks of savage fighting, the combatants agreed on a U.S.-brokered cease-fire.

At this point in the Lebanese Civil War, Ariel Sharon, now Israeli defense minister, concluded that the only solution to the continuing Katyusha threat was to drive the PLO out of Lebanon altogether. He used the lull in the fighting to plan a new incursion into Lebanon and waited for just the right time to implement it. That time arrived on June 3, 1982. Radical members of Fatah tried to assassinate the Israeli ambassador to Great Britain. Sharon had the excuse he needed.

Israel immediately launched retaliatory air strikes against PLO facilities in Beirut, killing more than 200 people. Two hours later, the Palestinians rained Katyusha rockets down on northern Israel. The fragile cease-fire of 1981 exploded with the rockets. Israeli forces entered Lebanon again on June 6.

Israelis called their latest foray "Operation Peace for Galilee." Their aim was to create a 25-mile neutral zone to protect their northern settlements.

UNIFIL troops were powerless to stop the Israeli advance. A UNIFIL press officer reported: "They were facing so little opposition that they did not bother with a combat formation. In Naqoura alone, we counted twelve hundred tanks and four thousand armored personnel carriers. God knows what else was pouring in. If a tank braked in Tyre, they were backed up all the way to Nahariya in Israel."[2] Israel ignored UN Security Council Resolution 509, issued that same day and demanding its immediate withdrawal.

In south Lebanon, militias guarding Palestinian refugee camps put up the strongest resistance against the advancing Israelis. Children as young as 13 or 14 fought the Israelis at close range with rocket-propelled grenades (RPGs). But they proved no match for Israeli artillery, air strikes, and tank fire. Many Lebanese—both Muslims and Christians—by contrast, greeted the invaders with handfuls of thrown rice.

By mid-July, more than 100,000 IDF troops had poured into Lebanon. They laid siege to Beirut, and in south Lebanon they dug in. The Israel Air Force wiped out Syrian air defenses and shot down dozens of Syrian MiGs in two days of fighting. But Syrian ground forces fought hard and blocked the IDF advance from reaching the crucial Beirut-Damascus highway that bisected the Bekaa Valley.

A few days later, Iran—already involved in a war with Iraq—sent several hundred Revolutionary Guards (known as *Pasdaran*) to the Bekaa Valley. "We are prepared to put our facilities and necessary training at the disposal of all Muslims who are prepared to fight against the Zionist regime,"[3] declared Iranian President Ali Khamenei. By the time the Pasdaran reached their destination, the fighting had ended.

In August, Philip Habib, U.S. special envoy to the Middle East, negotiated an end to the fighting. The agreement called for the evacuation of PLO and Syrian fighters from Beirut. It also provided for a Multinational Force (MNF) to oversee the withdrawal of the PLO. The MNF began arriving in Lebanon later that month. PLO leader Yasser Arafat and some 8,000 fighters left Beirut and headed for Tunisia. Most would eventually find their way back to the Israeli-controlled West Bank and Gaza Strip.

On September 14, a bomb blast killed Lebanese President-elect Bashir Gemayel, son of Phalangist founder Pierre Gemayel. Phalangist fighters rushed to avenge his death. "Bashir's death was immediately avenged by Christian partisans who entered Sabra and Shatila Palestinian refugee camps in Beirut's southern suburb," writes Hezbollah expert Judith Palmer Harik, "and between 16 and 18 September machine-gunned at least 1,500 men, women, and children and anything else that moved—dogs, horses, sheep—to death."[4] Bashir's elder brother Amine was elected president.

Meanwhile, in the Bekaa Valley, several loosely knit Lebanese groups with pro-Iranian leanings joined forces with a breakaway group from the Shia Amal Movement, led by a former chemistry teacher named Hussein al-Mussawi. Together, they formed an umbrella group searching for a name.

Hassan Nasrallah, the new group's future secretary-general, noted, "We were a young movement wanting to resist a legendary army [the IDF]. . . . The need was for men with the spirit of **jihad**, self-sacrifice, and endless giving. The only name that befits a group born with such motivations and spirit . . . is the name of *Hezbollah*."[5]

Terrorism

The Iranian Revolution

In 1921, cavalry officer Reza Khan overthrew the corrupt Qajar dynasty in Persia (renamed Iran in 1935). Khan changed his family name to Pahlavi. As Reza Shah Pahlavi, he established the Pahlavi dynasty in 1925. He improved transportation and communications systems and began a Westernization program. Reza abdicated his throne in 1941. He was succeeded by his son Mohammad Reza Shah Pahlavi.

In the 1950s, the young shah struck a deal with an eight-company oil cartel that guaranteed Iran a greater margin of profit than anywhere else in the Middle East. During the early 1960s, he introduced a series of economic and social reforms, while solidifying his grip on power. Upper-class Iranians prospered, but few benefits filtered down to the ordinary citizen. Many conservative Muslims felt that the shah's modernization programs violated traditional Islamic teachings. Unrest began to stir among his detractors.

"The powerful Iranian Shiite clergy (*mullahs*) decried the country's growing dependency on the USA," writes Judith Palmer Harik, "and viewed with concern the growing influence of America's secular culture on Iranian society."[6]

One of the mullahs, Ayatollah Ruhollah Khomeini, led the popular resistance to the shah and forced him to seek refuge abroad. Khomeini established an Islamic republic in Iran on April 1, 1979.

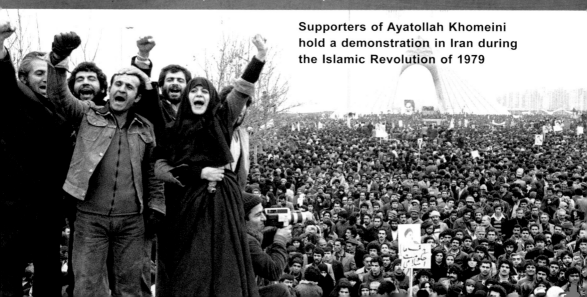

Supporters of Ayatollah Khomeini hold a demonstration in Iran during the Islamic Revolution of 1979

Marines of the multinational peacekeeping force in Lebanon view the damage to the U.S. Embassy in Beirut in April, 1983. The massive blast, caused by a suicide bomber, killed 63 people, including 17 Americans.

CHAPTER 4
The Rise of Hezbollah

Hezbollah, according to Shia cleric and former Iranian minister of the interior Ali Akbar Mohtashami, is "the spiritual child of Imam Khomeini and the Islamic Revolution."[1] Mohtashami is "seen as a founder of the Hezbollah movement in Lebanon."[2] Many people refer to him as "Hizballah's **midwife**."[3] Other founders included Raghib Harb, Mohammad Hussein Fadlallah, Ibrahim al-Amin, Abbas al-Mussawi, Subhi al-Tufayli, and Hussein Mussawi.

The new organization received help from the Pasdaran who had arrived in the Bekaa Valley. Training by Iran's Islamic Revolutionary Guard left its mark on the impressionable Lebanese youth. As Hezbollah co-founder Abbas al-Mussawi observed, the Guard inspired a new brand of terror: "[The Pasdaran] made the Muslim youths love martyrdom. And so we were not surprised at all when, shortly after the arrival of the Guards, a Muslim youth in Lebanon smiled at death while carrying with him 1,200 kilograms [about 2,650 pounds] of explosives."[4]

Suicide bombing soon became the signature terror dispenser of Hezbollah operatives. In 1983, Hezbollah suicide bombers blasted their way onto the world stage in attempts to seek a **martyr's** reward in paradise. Since their inception, however, they have never claimed responsibility for their attacks. Hezbollah prefers to operate under a variety of aliases, such as Islamic Jihad, the Cells of the Armed Struggle, Ansar Allah, the Partisans of God, and more.

On April 18, 1983, a spectacular car-bomb attack on the U.S. Embassy in Beirut killed 63 people, including 17 Americans. It

marked the beginning of Islamist terror attacks on Americans. The Islamic Jihad claimed responsibility for the attack, but blame was later attributed to Hezbollah and Iran. Hezbollah followed up their embassy bombing with the ruinous attack on the Marine barracks in October.

Mohammad Hussein Fadlallah, the group's spiritual leader, denied any direct involvement by Hezbollah in the barracks bombing. He did, however, assert that "the Muslims believe that you struggle by transforming yourself into a living bomb like you struggle with a gun in your hand. There is no difference between dying with a gun in your hand or exploding yourself."[5]

In the wake of the Beirut bombings, the Western powers withdrew their peacekeeping troops in the Multinational Force early in 1984. Arabs and Muslims everywhere interpreted the U.S. withdrawal in the face of terror as a sign of America's weakness. They claimed victory for their doctrine of armed struggle and confrontation. Friends and enemies alike concluded that America was not an ally to rely on.

On September 20, 1984, Hezbollah attacked the U.S. Embassy annex in Beirut with a car bomb, killing two Americans and 22 others. Throughout the rest of the 1980s, the group broadened its activities to include attacks against Westerners in Lebanon— mainly Americans, French, Germans, and Jews. It also added kidnapping, hijacking, and murder to its growing portfolio of terror tactics.

By the end of 1984, Israel was facing deepening troubles in Lebanon. Beirut had fallen to the militias after the departure of the MNF, and the Lebanese army had pretty much dissolved. In the south, Major Saad Haddad, Israel's greatest ally, died of cancer. His northern replacement lacked the support of the South Lebanese Army. Worse yet, both the Israeli military and civilian populations were becoming disenchanted with the long and seemingly unending Israeli presence in Lebanon.

"You see the change first of all in the eyes of the soldiers," observed Zeev Schiff, military correspondent for Israel's *Haaretz* newspaper. "It's a look that reminded me of the look in the eyes of the American soldiers I saw in the final stages of Vietnam. It is the look of soldiers and officers who know that their chances of winning in Lebanon are less than zero."[6] Early in January 1985, Israel announced plans to withdraw to the old Haddad Security Zone that existed from 1979 to 1982.

The following month, after many months of denying responsibility for its actions, Hezbollah issued a public declaration of its

Sheikh Mohammad Fadlallah, wearing a black turban and surrounded by his defiant bodyguards, approaches a mosque in Beirut's southern suburbs to attend a funeral for 75 victims of a car-bomb explosion. The blast occurred just a few yards from Fadlallah's home in the Ghobeiri suburb of Beirut, but the leader of Hezbollah—or God's Party—escaped the explosion without injury.

principles and policies. Its charter took the form of a 48-page open letter to the "Downtrodden in Lebanon and in the World." The document expressed Hezbollah's fidelity to Ayatollah Khomeini and identified its primary enemies as the United States and Israel: "We see in Israel the vanguard of the United States in our Islamic world. It is the hated enemy that must be fought until the hated ones get what they deserve. . . . Therefore our struggle will end only when this entity [Israel] is obliterated."[7]

Hezbollah's growing popularity brought it into violent conflict with the Amal Movement. Hezbollah wanted free access to south Lebanon to pursue its fight against Israel. Amal considered Hezbollah's presence as an encroachment on its sole remaining bastion. Beginning in 1988, the two factions engaged in occasional skirmishes. Minor clashes soon escalated into open war. More than a thousand combatants and civilians were killed in a struggle filled with atrocities and assassinations. Hezbollah generally prevailed in the fighting, but Syrian intervention usually denied it the winner's spoils.

In October, 1989, the Lebanon National Assembly met in Taif, Saudi Arabia, and—with the help of Saudi Arabia, the United States, and Syria—endorsed an agreement for national reconciliation called the Taif Agreement. It shifted governmental power away from the Maronite presidency to a cabinet divided equally between Muslims and Christians.

Further, the Taif Agreement mapped out a security plan that extended government sovereignty over all Lebanese territory and provided for the disarming of all militias. It also called for a withdrawal of Syrian forces, and a Syria-Lebanon arrangement to bring about the withdrawal of Israeli forces from Lebanese territory.

Israel finally withdrew its forces in May, 2000, except for a small disputed sector known as Shebaa Farms. The Lebanese Civil War was over. Hezbollah was allowed to keep its arms as a "resistance force" rather than a militia. It remains armed to this day.

Prime Targets

Between January, 1982 and August, 1988, Hezbollah accounted for 51 of 96 international kidnappings. The group acted "under the assumed strict control and direction of Iran's clerical establishment,"[8] according to terrorism authority Matthew Leavitt. Hezbollah, if not directed by Iran, was at least influenced by it. Americans received special attention.

On March 16, 1984, Hezbollah terrorists kidnapped William Buckley, CIA station chief in Beirut, and tortured him to death. They delivered his remains in a plastic bag on the side of an airport road in 1991.

The following year, Hezbollah members hijacked TWA Flight 847 from Athens to Rome and forced it to land in Beirut. Singling out U.S. Navy diver Robert Stetham, they executed him and dumped his body on the tarmac. They released all the other passengers without harming them.

On February 17, 1988, Marine Lt. Col. William Higgins was abducted while returning from a routine liaison meeting with an Amal leader in south Lebanon. Higgins headed a 76-man UN observer group. A brown Volvo intercepted his white, UN-marked Jeep Wagoneer on a potholed coastal road south of Tyre. Armed Hezbollah operatives dragged Higgins out of his car into the Volvo and sped off. His remains were recovered nearly four years later.

Based on these and other attacks in the 1980s and 1990s against Americans and other Western targets, the U.S. government declared Hezbollah a Foreign Terrorist Organization (FTO) in October, 1997.

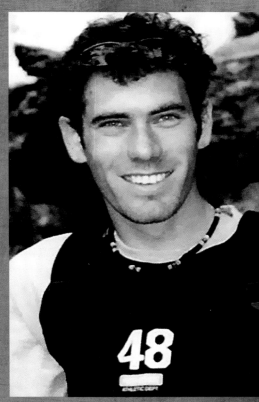

Israeli reserve soldier Eldad Regev is one of two Israeli army reservists who were captured and killed by Lebanese Hezbollah militia in a cross-border raid on July 12, 2006.

On Wednesday, July 12, 2006, Hezbollah militants launched a cross-border raid into Israel and captured two Israeli soldiers. The attack triggered an Israeli attack on Lebanon with warplanes, gunboats, and soldiers to search for the captives. The ensuing violence took the lives of two Lebanese and seven Israeli soldiers. An Israeli artillery unit (shown here) on the frontier at Zaura, in northern Israel, fires across the border into Lebanon in retaliation.

CHAPTER 5
Time and Tussle

After Israel's withdrawal from southern Lebanon, Hezbollah fighters took control of the vacated area. Lebanese security forces and UN peacekeepers moved into most of southern Lebanon by September. Hezbollah kept control of the area closest to the Israel-Lebanon border and continued to harass the Israelis with sporadic cross-border raids.

Syria maintained its forces in Lebanon. On February 14, 2005, Rafic Hariri, a former Lebanese prime minister and a member of the anti-Syrian opposition, was killed by a car bomb in Beirut. Twenty-one others died in the blast. Hezbollah was suspected of the assassination but denied any responsibility. Anti-Syrian demonstrators took to the streets for two weeks. Under growing pressure from Lebanese citizens and the urgings of foreign nations, Syria withdrew all of its forces from Lebanon two months later.

On July 12, 2006, Hezbollah fighters attacked an Israeli army post with rifle fire and RPGs. The raiders killed eight Israeli soldiers and abducted two more as prisoners of war. Hezbollah hoped to barter for the release of a number of Israeli-held prisoners. Upon hearing of the attack, senior Israeli military officials began to threaten that the "period of quiet is over." They refused to negotiate and said that if the kidnapped soldiers were not released "we'll turn Lebanon's clock back twenty years."[1]

Israel retaliated with a major military offensive against Hezbollah, touching off what became known as the Second Lebanon War. Israel's powerful response surprised Hezbollah's leader, Hassan Nasrallah. He had not expected such a strong

Israeli reaction, but he quickly rose to the challenge. "You wanted an open war, an open war is what you will get," he said two days later. "It will be a full-scale war. To Haifa and—believe me—beyond Haifa and beyond beyond Haifa."[2] Hezbollah fired thousands of rockets into Israel.

The war ended on August 14, when both sides accepted the provisions of UN Security Council Resolution 1701 for a cease-fire. During its 34 days, the conflict claimed the lives of 43 Israeli and more than 1,100 Lebanese civilians. Military deaths numbered 118 Israeli and 28 Lebanese soldiers, and about 200 Hezbollah fighters. The war displaced about a half-million Israelis

In July, 2008, members of the Hezbollah community gather in the southern suburbs of Beirut, Lebanon, to pray over the coffins of eight militants killed in the 2006 war. The war killed more than 1,200 people in Lebanon. Following an exchange agreement between Israel and Lebanon, Israel recovered the bodies of two Israeli soldiers, who have since been buried. In return, Israel freed five prisoners, including four Hezbollah fighters captured in the war. The five captives were the last Lebanese remaining in Israeli jails.

from northern Israel, and emptied southern Lebanon of its civilian population of some 900,000 people. Material losses totaled approximately $500 million in Israel and about $4 billion in Lebanon. Both sides claimed victory in a war without winners.

Hezbollah forces had proven to be a far more formidable adversary than Israel had anticipated. They fought the Israel Defense Forces to a standstill—something no other Arab militia had ever achieved. Its credible showing against the IDF elevated Hezbollah, and its leader, Hassan Nasrallah, as heroes across the Arab world. In the months after its conflict with Israel, Hezbollah tried unsuccessfully to use its new prestige to gain **veto** power in the Lebanese Cabinet.

In May, 2008, Hezbollah forces clashed with government supporters in Beirut over government decisions that included plans to dismantle Hezbollah's communications network. Hezbollah runs a satellite television station, al-Manar TV ("the Lighthouse"), and a radio station, al-Nour ("the Light"). It also publishes a newspaper, al Ahd ("the Promise"). The group's leader, Nasrallah, viewed the government's decision as a declaration of war. He mobilized Hezbollah's armed forces and quickly seized control of parts of Beirut.

The government soon backed away from the decisions that had sparked the outbreak of violence. In a summit held in Doha, Qatar, on May 21, 2008, both factions signed a pact known as the Doha Agreement. The agreement granted Hezbollah its long-sought veto power: 11 of 30 seats in a newly formed unity government.

On August 4, 2008, Lebanon's new Cabinet unanimously approved a draft resolution recognizing Hezbollah's existence as an armed organization and guaranteeing its right "to liberate the Israeli-occupied Shebaa Farms, Kafar Shuba Hills, and the Lebanese section of Ghajar village, and defend the country using all legal and possible means."[3] In the eyes of the Western world,

Hezbollah's legitimacy as an armed resistance movement remains a matter of great controversy.

In 2009, Hezbollah won 10 seats in the Lebanese **parliament** in the national election in its continuing efforts to become a legitimate representative of the Lebanese people. On November 30, it announced a new political strategy in the form of a revised **manifesto**. Its new policy toned down the Islamic rhetoric but preserved a tough line toward Israel and the United States.

Hassan Nasrallah restated Hezbollah's rejection of an Israeli state: "This stand is firm, permanent, and final, and it does not tolerate any retreat or compromise even if the entire world recognizes Israel."[4]

Nasrallah had assumed the leadership of Hezbollah as secretary general in 1992, following the targeted killing of the group's co-founder, Abbas al-Mussawi, by Israeli agents. He was chosen by a seven-member **shura** council, which also oversees five sub-councils: 1) the political assembly, 2) jihad assembly, 3) parliamentary assembly, 4) executive assembly, and 5) judicial assembly.

Structurally, Hezbollah has a single leadership. It makes no distinction between its political and social activities within Lebanon, and its military jihadist actions against Israel. The same leadership directs all political, social, and military operations. Iran, according to U.S. estimates, funds Hezbollah's operations in amounts ranging from $60 to $100 million a year. Waging war against Israel, while struggling to win the confidence and favor of the Lebanese people, is costly. And the battles rage on.

In mid-2013, Nasrallah publicly vowed to support Bashar al-Assad's Syrian regime in its fight for survival. "This battle is ours . . . and I promise you victory,"[5] he declared. Thousands of Hezbollah Shia fighters have streamed eastward into Syria to combat Syrian rebels and fighters of the Islamic State, the former al-Qaeda in Iraq.

"The decision to send **expeditionary** forces to Syria marked a major turning point for Hezbollah, leaving southern Lebanon potentially exposed to Israel," writes political analyst Robert Danin. "This move has left many [Shia] in Lebanon worried that Hezbollah has overreached and forsaken its commitment to Lebanon in favor of its larger alliance with Iran and Assad's Syria."[6]

Hezbollah's commitment in Syria exacted a high cost. By the end of 2016, an estimated 1,700 of its fighters had been killed and thousands more wounded.

Syrian children at the Marj al-Khokh refugee camp, near Marjayoun village in southern Lebanon, shout slogans during a celebration of the recapture of the Syrian border town of Yarbroud by Syrian forces on March 18, 2014. Backed by Hezbollah fighters, the Syrian forces had driven the rebels out of Yarbroud and gained full control of the town two days earlier. Their victory helped to secure the land route connecting the capital Damascus with Aleppo, Syria's second largest city, and the Mediterranean Sea. The girl in the foreground holds pictures of Syria's President Bashar al-Assad (right) and Lebanon's Hezbollah leader Hassan Nasrallah.

On the other hand, with the winds of war seemingly shifting in favor of Assad's government forces and their allies in 2017, Hezbollah very well might emerge from the Syrian Civil War as its biggest winner. "While not unscathed, Hezbollah stands to gain momentum at home and throughout the region," according to political analysts Colin P. Clarke and Chad C. Serena of the RAND Corporation. "Through its evolution from ragtag militia to global terrorist organization and Lebanese political party, Hezbollah has cemented its status as a power player in the Middle East."[7]

Masked protestors in Srinagar, the summer capital of Indian-controlled Kashmir, burn pictures of Iranian President Hassan Rouhani, Lebanese Hezbollah chief Hassan Nasrallah, and Syrian President Bashar al-Assad during a demonstration against the three leaders on January 13, 2017. Srinagar activists violently protested the killing of civilians in Syria by Assad's forces. Indian police later dispersed the protestors with smoke shells and stun grenades.

Uncertain Future

Military analysts estimate as many as 8,000 Hezbollah Shia foot soldiers are fighting in Syria. They have played a vital role in rolling back some of the gains of opposition fighters. But the group's presence in Syria raises a question: What happens to Hezbollah if the regime of Bashar al-Assad falls?

"I don't think there's an assumption that it will be the end of Hezbollah," writes Lebanese commentator Michael Young. "Hezbollah's capacity to engage in war will be much diminished; it will not have the same ability to re-arm itself and it won't have this big ally sitting on the Lebanese border that can help it."[8] A weakened ability to replenish itself could prove critical to Hezbollah going forward.

Israeli General Benny Gantz points out that Hezbollah's attention is divided between domestic politics, military preparations against Israel, and its intervention in Syria. So far, the mutual fear of another damaging war has kept the peace. "Hezbollah is like a state and they know exactly what is going to happen in Lebanon if they start a war with us," Gantz said, "and that this would set Lebanon back decades."[9]

Despite Hezbollah's losses in Syria, few would deny that it has gained valuable combat experience in the civil war. It has become more proficient at mass maneuver and coordination with other allied groups on the battlefield. And it has learned to use artillery cover and reconnaissance and surveillance drones more effectively, while improving its logistical operations in support of large-scale offensives. "In some ways, Syria is a dress rehearsal for our next war with Israel,"[10] a Hezbollah special forces commander admitted to VOA (Voice of America) News in 2016. Today, many observers believe another war with Israel lies just over the horizon. Going forward in 2017, the unresolved Israel-Hezbollah question faces an uncertain future at best.

TIMELINE

c. 325 Christians arrive in Lebanon.

638 Muslims arrive in Lebanon.

1095 Crusades begin; they end in 1291.

1299 Ottoman Empire founded; it ends in 1922.

1516 Ottomans conquer Lebanon.

1914 World War I begins; it ends in 1918.

1921 Reza Khan overthrows the corrupt Qajar dynasty in Persia.

1923 League of Nations grants France a mandate for Syria and Lebanon.

1925 Reza Shah Pahlavi establishes the Pahlavi dynasty.

1943 Lebanon gains independence from France.

1958 Muslims rebel against Lebanese government. U.S. sends Marine contingent to Lebanon in July; they leave in October.

1964 Palestine Liberation Organization (PLO) is founded in Jerusalem.

1969 Lebanon and PLO sign Cairo Agreement.

1974 Musa al-Sadr founds the Movement of the Dispossessed. Israeli incursions into Lebanon begin.

1975 Musa al-Sadr launches the Amal Movement, the military wing of the Movement of the Dispossessed. Lebanese Civil War begins; it ends in 1990.

1976 Syrian troops known as the Arab Deterrent Force (ADF) enter Lebanon in June.

1978 Operation Litani begins on March 18 following Fatah terrorist attack; it ends six days later. United Nations (UN) adopt Resolutions 425 and 426. Phalangists kill Tony Frangieh in June. Musa al-Sadr disappears mysteriously while visiting Libya in August.

1979 Iranian ruler Mohammad Reza Shah Pahlavi flees his throne on January 16; Islamic Republic created on April 1; Ayatollah Ruhollah Khomeini becomes supreme leader.

1981 PLO and Israel Defense Forces clash in July-August.

1982 Hezbollah is founded in Lebanon. "Operation Peace for Galilee" begins on June 4; it ends in June, 1985. Multinational Force arrives in Lebanon on August 1. Bomb blast kills Lebanese President-elect Bashir Gemayel on September 14. Pasdaran arrive in the Bekaa Valley to train Hezbollah fighters.

1983 Hezbollah terrorists drive explosive-laden vehicles into Marine barracks and French paratrooper barracks in Beirut.

1984 Hezbollah kidnaps William Buckley on March 16. Hezbollah attacks U.S. Embassy annex in Beirut with car bomb on September 20.

1985 Israel announces plans to withdraw to the Security Zone on January 14. Hezbollah issues a public declaration of its principles and policies on February 16. Hezbollah members hijack TWA Flight 847 on June 14.

1988 Hezbollah abducts Lt. Col. William Higgins on February 17.

1992 Hassan Nasrallah assumes leadership of Hezbollah.

2000 Israel withdraws forces from Lebanon.

2005 Rafic Hariri is killed by a car bomb in Beirut on February 14.

2006 Hezbollah fighters launch a military operation against Israel on July 12, leading to Second Lebanon War; fighting ends on August 14.

2008 Hezbollah forces clash with government supporters in Beirut in May. Lebanon's Cabinet unanimously recognizes Hezbollah's existence as an armed organization on August 4.

2009 Hezbollah wins ten parliamentary seats; announces a new political strategy on November 30.

2013 Nasrallah publicly vows support for Bashar al-Assad's Syrian regime.

2014 Hezbollah forces fight on the al-Nusra Front alongside Syrian Army in battle for Yabroud.

2015 Many Hezbollah fighters refuse to serve further in Syria over mounting losses.

2016 Aleppo, Syria's second-largest city, falls to Syrian government forces, aided by Hezbollah militants and Russian air strikes.

2017 Hezbollah's presence in Syria enhances its role as a power player in the Middle East going forward.

CHAPTER NOTES

Chapter 1   Cast in Fire

1. David Evins, "Navy-Marine Corps Team in Lebanon." *Proceedings.* May 1984. http://www.navalhistory.org/2013/10/23/beirut-marine-barracks-bombing-october-23-1983

2. Jim Michaels, "Recalling the deadly 1983 attack on the Marine barracks." *USA Today.* October 23, 2013. http://usatoday.com/story/nation/2013/10/23/marines-beirut-lebanon-hezbollah/3171593/

3. Betty Radice, ed., *The Koran.* Penguin Classics. Translated with notes by N. L. Dawood (New York: Penguin Books, 1977), 58:22, p. 273.

4. James Phillips, "The 1983 Marine Barracks Bombing: Connecting the Dots." *The Daily Signal.* October 23, 2009. http://dailysignal.com/print/?post_id=17927

5. Matthew Levitt, *Hezbollah: The Global Footprint of Lebanon's Party of God* (Washington, DC: Georgetown University Press, 2013), p. 11.

6. Ibid., p. 12.

Chapter 2   Raison D'être

1. Nicholas Blanford, *Warriors of God: Inside Hezbollah's Thirty-Year Struggle against Israel* (New York: Random House, 2011), p. 19.

2. Ibid., p. 23.

3. Pierre Tristem, "Israel's 1978 Invasion of Lebanon." http://middleeast.about.com/od/lebanon/a/me080316b.htm

Chapter 3   In God's Name

1. "AROUND THE WORLD; Khomeini Urges Export of Iranian Revolution." *The New York Times.* October 15, 1981. http://www.nytimes.com/1981/10/15/world/around-the-world-khomeini-urges-export-of-iranian-revolution.html

2. Nicholas Blanford, *Warriors of God: Inside Hezbollah's Thirty-Year Struggle against Israel* (New York: Random House, 2011), p. 41.

3. Ibid., p. 43.

4. Judith Palmer Harik, *Hezbollah: The Changing Face of Terrorism* (London, UK: I. B. Tauris, 2007), p. 35.

5. Joshua L. Gleis and Benedetta Berti, *Hezbollah and Hamas: A Comparative Study* (Baltimore, MD: The Johns Hopkins University Press, 2012), p. 39.

6. Harik, *Hezbollah*, p. 15.

Chapter 4   The Rise of Hezbollah

1. Dominque Avon and Anaïs-Trissa Khatchadourian, *Hezbollah: A History of the "Party of God."* Translated by Jane Marie Todd (Cambridge, MA: Harvard University Press, 2012), p. 25.

2. BBC News. "Iranian publisher defies court." BBC News. June 26, 2000. http://news.bbc.co.uk/2/hi/middle_east/806698.stm

3. Yehudit Barsky, "Terrorism Briefing: Hizballah." The American Jewish Committee. http://www.ajc.org/atf/cf/%7B42D75369-D582-4380-8395-D25925B85EAF%7D/Hizballah_052003.pdf

4. Ibid.

5. Ibid.

6. Nicholas Blanford, *Warriors of God: Inside Hezbollah's Thirty-Year Struggle against Israel* (New York: Random House, 2011), p. 67.

7. Council on Foreign Relations, "An Open Letter: The Hizballah Program." Council on Foreign Relations. January 1, 1988. http://www.cfr.org/terrorist-organizations-and-networks/open-letter-hizballah-program/p30967

8. Matthew Levitt, *Hezbollah: The Global Footprint of Lebanon's Party of God* (Washington, DC: Georgetown University Press, 2013), p. 34.

Chapter 5   Time and Tussle

1. Nicholas Blanford, *Warriors of God: Inside Hezbollah's Thirty-Year Struggle against Israel* (New York: Random House, 2011), p. 378.

2. Ibid., p. 372.

3. Nafez Qawas, "Berri summons Parliament to vote on policy statement." *The Daily Star*. Lebanon. August 6, 2008. http://www.dailystar.com.lb/ArticlePrint.aspx?id=50807&mode=print

4. Jonathan Masters and Zachary Laub, "Hezbollah (a.k.a. Hizbollah, Hizbu'llah)." Council on Foreign Relations. January 3, 2014. http://www.cfr.org/lebanon/hezbollah-k-hizbollah-hisbullaqh/p9155

5. Ibid.

6. Ibid.

7. Colin P. Clarke and Chad C. Serene, "Hezbollah Is Winning the War in Syria." *The National Interest*. January 29, 2017. http://nationalinterest.org/feature/hezbollah-winning-the-war-syria-19229

8. Jamie Detmer, "Lebanon Faces Uncertain Future if Assad Falls." Voice of America News. July 8, 2013. http://www.voanews.com/articleprintview/1697054.html

9. Nicholas Blanford, "Israel: Hezbollah is now stronger than any Arab army." *The Christian Science Monitor*. June 9, 2014. http://www.csmonitor.com/World/Middle-East/2014/0609/Israel-Hezbollah-is-now- stronger-than-any-Arab-army

10. Jamie Detmer, "Hezbollah Develops New Skills in Syria, Posing Challenges for Israel." Voice of America News. April 27, 2016. http://www.voanews.com/a/hezbollah-develops-new-skills-in-syria-posing-challenges-for-israel/3304664.html

PRINCIPAL PEOPLE

Ibrahim al-Amin (IB-ruh-heem al-uh-MEEN)—Amal's representative to Iran.

Yasser Arafat (YAS-suhr ar-uh-FAT)—leader of the Palestinian Liberation Organization and the Palestine Authority.

Bashar al-Assad (bah-SHAHR al-AH-sahd)—president of Syria since 2000.

Camille Chamoun (kuh-MEEL sham-OON)—president of Lebanon from 1952 to 1958; a leading Christian leader during most of the Lebanese Civil War.

Mohammad Hussein Fadlallah (moh-HAH-mehd hoo-SAYN fahd-LAH-lah)—spiritual mentor of Hezbollah.

Suleiman Frangieh (SOO-luh-man FRAN-ji-yeh)—president of Lebanon from 1970 to 1976 and a Christian warlord.

Bashir Gemayel (buh-SHEER ju-MY-yel)—Lebanese politician, militia leader, and president-elect; son of Pierre Gemayel.

Pierre Gemayel (pee-AIR ju-MY-yel)—Lebanese political leader and founder of the Phalange Party.

Philip Habib (FIL-ip ha-BEEB)—U.S. special envoy to the Middle East.

Saad Haddad (SAHD had-AD)—founder and head of the South Lebanese Army (SLA).

Raghib Harb (ruh-GHEEB HARB)—Lebanese resistance leader and Muslim cleric.

Rafic Hariri (rah-FEEK hah-REE-ree)—prime minister of Lebanon (1992–1998; 2000–2004).

Ali Khamenei (ah-LEE kha-MAY-nee)— Supreme leader of Iran since 1989.

Ayatollah Ruhollah Khomeini (eye-uh-TOLL-ah roo-hoh-LAH koh-MAYN-ee)—supreme leader of Iran (1979–1989).

Ali Akbar Mohtashami (AL-ee AK-bahr moh-tuh-SHAM-ee)—minister of the interior of Iran (1985–1989).

Dalal Mughrabi (duh-LAHL moo-GRAY-bee)—Fatah female leader of the terrorist attack known as the Coastal Road Massacre.

Abbas al-Mussawi (ab-BAHS al-MOO-suh-wee)—Shia cleric; co-founder and Secretary General of Hezbollah (1991–1992).

Hussein al-Mussawi (hoo-SAYN al-MOO-suh-wee)—Lebanese Shia; founder of the Amal Movement.

Hassan Nasrallah (HASS-ahn naz-RAHL-lah)—secretary general of Hezbollah.

Mohammad Reza Shah Pahlavi (moh-HAH-mehd ri-ZUH shuh pa-leh-VEE)—shah of Iran (1941–1979).

Musa al-Sadr (MOO-sah al-SAD-er)—Iranian-born Shia cleric; founder and leader of the Movement of the Dispossessed and its military wing Amal.

Ariel Sharon (ah-REE-ehl sha-RONE)—prime minister of Israel (2001–2006); defense minister of Israel (1981–1983).

Subhi al-Tufayli (SOOB-hee al-tu-FAY-lee)—Shia Islamist and secretary general of Hezbollah (1989–1991).

Ezer Weizman (EE-zer VIZE-man)—Israeli minister of defense and seventh president of Israel.

GLOSSARY

coerce (coe-ERSS)—obtain something by using force or the threat of force

dissidents (DISS-uh-dents)—people who oppose an official policy

emancipation (uh-man-suh-PAY-shun—liberation; process of being set free

expeditionary (ek-speh-DISH-uh-ner-ee)—sent on a military operation

ideological (i-di-oh-LOJ-i-kal)—referring to the ideas that form the basis of an economic or political theory

Islam (IS-lahm, or is-LAHM)—the Muslim religion, based on the teachings of the Prophet Muhammad; the Muslim world

jihad (jih-HAHD)—Arabic for to strive or struggle (in the path of God); holy war

Katyusha (kat-YEW-shuh) rocket—Russian surface-to-surface missile built in a variety of calibers

League of Nations (LEEG of NAY-shuns)—organization for international cooperation and prevention of war formed after World War I

mandate (MAN-dayt)—authority to perform a certain task or apply certain policies

manifesto (man-ih-FES-toh)—a public declaration of principles and policy

martyr (MAHR-tihr)—a person who suffers death rather than give up a religious faith; one who undergoes death or great suffering in support of a belief or cause or principle

midwife (MIHD-wife)—person who assists in childbirth

militia (muh-LIH-shuh)—military group that isn't part of a country's official armed forces

parliament (PAHR-luh-ment)—an assembly that makes the laws of certain countries

precursor (pree-CUHR-suhr)—something that comes before something else

primeval (pry-MEE-vuhl)—the earliest ages in world history

profane (proh-FANE)—disrespectful of religious practice

secular (SEK-yew-lahr)—concerned with worldly affairs rather than spiritual ones; an opposition to or rejection of religion

Shia (SHEE-uh)—Along with Sunni, one of the two major divisions of Islam; a Muslim who adheres to its principles; worldwide they compose about 10–15 percent of Muslims; also known as Shiites

shura (SHOO-ruh)—consultation; council; elective process

theocracy (thee-AH-cruh-see)—state governed by divine guidance or by officials regarded as divinely guided

veto (VEE-toh)—an authoritative rejection of something that is proposed; the right to make such a rejection

FURTHER READING

Burgan, Michael. *Terrorist Groups*. North Mankato, MN: Compass Point Books, 2010.

Byers, Ann. *Lebanon's Hezbollah*. New York: Rosen Publishing Group, 2003.

Kort, Michael G. *The Handbook of the Middle East*. The Handbook Of . . . Series. Minneapolis, MN: Twenty-First Century Books, 2007.

Landau, Elaine. *Suicide Bombers: Foot Soldiers of the Terrorist Movement*. Minneapolis, MN: Twenty-First Century Books, 2006.

Tougas, Shelley. *What Makes a Terrorist?* North Mankato, MN: Compass Point Books, 2010.

WORKS CONSULTED

"AROUND THE WORLD; Khomeini Urges Export of Iranian Revolution." *The New York Times*. October 15, 1981. http://www.nytimes.com/1981/10/15/world/around-the-world-khomeini-urges-export-of-iranian-revolution.html

Avon, Dominque, and Anaïs-Trissa Khatchadourian. *Hezbollah: A History of the "Party of God."* Translated by Jane Marie Todd. Cambridge, MA: Harvard University Press, 2012.

Barsky, Yehudit. "Terrorism Briefing: Hizballah." The American Jewish Committee. http://www.ajc.org/atf/cf/%7B42D75369-D582-4380-8395-D25925B85EAF%7D/Hizballah_052003.pdf

Blanford, Nicholas. "Israel: Hezbollah is now stronger than any Arab army." *The Christian Science Monitor*. June 9, 2014. http://www.csmonitor.com/World/Middle-East/2014/0609/Israel-Hezbollah-is-now-stronger-than-any-Arab-army

———. *Warriors of God: Inside Hezbollah's Thirty-Year Struggle against Israel*. New York: Random House, 2011.

Campo, Juan E., ed. *Encyclopedia of Islam*. New York: Checkmark Books, 2009.

Clarke, Colin P., and Chad C. Serene. "Hezbollah Is Winning the War in Syria." *The National Interest*. January 29, 2017. http://nationalinterest.org/feature/hezbollah-winning-the-war-syria-19229

Council on Foreign Relations. "An Open Letter: The Hizballah Program." Council on Foreign Relations. January 1, 1988. http://www.cfr.org/terrorist-organizations-and-networks/open-letter-hizballah-program/p30967

Detmer, Jamie. "Hezbollah Develops New Skills in Syria, Posing Challenges for Israel." Voice of America News. April 27, 2016. http://www.voanews.com/a/hezbollah-develops-new-skills-in-syria-posing-challenges-for-israel/3304664.html

———. "Lebanon Faces Uncertain Future if Assad Falls." Voice of America News. July 8, 2013. http://www.voanews.com/a/lebanon-faces-uncertain-future-if-assad-falls/1697054.html

Evins, David. "Navy-Marine Corps Team in Lebanon." *Proceedings*. May 1984. http://www.navalhistory.org/2013/10/23/beirut-marine-barracks-bombing-october-23-1983

WORKS CONSULTED

Gleis, Joshua L., and Benedetta Berti. *Hezbollah and Hamas: A Comparative Study*. Baltimore, MD: The Johns Hopkins University Press, 2012.

Harik, Judith Palmer. *Hezbollah: The Changing Face of Terrorism*. London, UK: I. B. Tauris, 2007.

"Iranian publisher defies court." BBC News. June 26, 2000. http://news.bbc.co.uk/2/hi/middle_east/806698.stm

Levitt, Matthew. *Hezbollah: The Global Footprint of Lebanon's Party of God*. Washington, DC: Georgetown University Press, 2013.

Masters, Jonathan, and Zachary Laub. "Hezbollah (a.k.a. Hizbollah, Hizbu'llah)." Council on Foreign Relations. January 3, 2014. http://www.cfr.org/lebanon/hezbollah-k-hizbollah-hisbullah/p9155

Michaels, Jim. "Recalling the deadly 1983 attack on the Marine barracks." *USA Today*. October 23, 2013. http://usatoday.com/story/nation/2013/10/23/marines-beirut-lebanon-hezbollah/3171593/

Norton, Augustus Richard. *Hezbollah: A Short History*. Princeton, NJ: Princeton University Press, 2007.

Phillips, James. "The 1983 Marine Barracks Bombing: Connecting the Dots." *The Daily Signal*. October 23, 2009. http://dailysignal.com/print/?post_id=17927

Qawas, Nafez. "Berri summons Parliament to vote on policy statement." *The Daily Star*. Lebanon. August 6, 2008. http://www.dailystar.com.lb/ArticlePrint.aspx?id=50807&mode=print

Radice, Betty, ed. *The Koran*. Penguin Classics. Translated with notes by N. L. Dawood. New York: Penguin Books, 1977.

Sela, Avraham. *The Continuum Political Encyclopedia of the Middle East*. Revised and Updated Ed. New York: Continuum, 2002.

Totten, Michael J. *The Road to Fatima Gate: The Beirut Spring, the Rise of Hezbollah, and the Iranian War against Israel*. New York: Encounter Books, 2012.

Tristem, Pierre. "Israel's 1978 Invasion of Lebanon." http://middleeast.about.com/od/lebanon/a/me080316b.htm

ON THE INTERNET

Council on Foreign Relations. "An Open Letter: The Hizballah Program." http://cfr.org/terrorist-organizations-and-networks/open-letter-hizballah-program/p30967

Levitt, Matthew. "30 Years Later: The Marine Barracks Bombing and the Birth of Hezbollah." Defense One. October 23, 2013. http://www.defenseone.com/threats/2013/10/30-years-later-marine-barracks-bombing-and-birth-hezbollah/72512/

United Against Nuclear Iran. "The Iranian Regime Terrorism Timeline." http://www.unitedagainstnucleariran.com/terrorism

INDEX